INDEX

DIFFICULTY LEVEL	Important Notes	PG.NO

INDEX 

DIFFICULTY LEVEL	Important Notes	PG.NO

REVISION

QUESTIONS CAN BE ASK

MAIN

KEYWORDS

REVISION

 DO 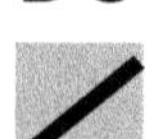 IT 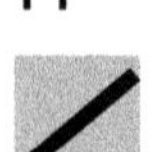

MAIN

KEYWORDS

  DO  IT   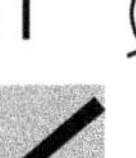 

QUESTIONS CAN BE ASK

MAIN

KEYWORDS

REVISION

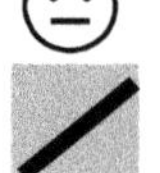 DO  IT 

MAIN

KEYWORDS

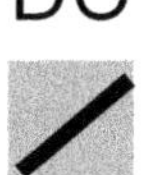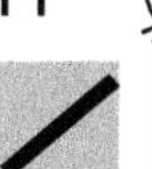

REVISION

QUESTIONS CAN BE ASK

MAIN

KEYWORDS

REVISION
DO IT
QUESTIONS CAN BE ASK
MAIN
KEYWORDS

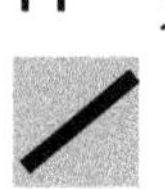

REVISION

QUESTIONS CAN BE ASK

MAIN

KEYWORDS

QUESTIONS CAN BE ASK

MAIN

KEYWORDS

QUESTIONS CAN BE ASK

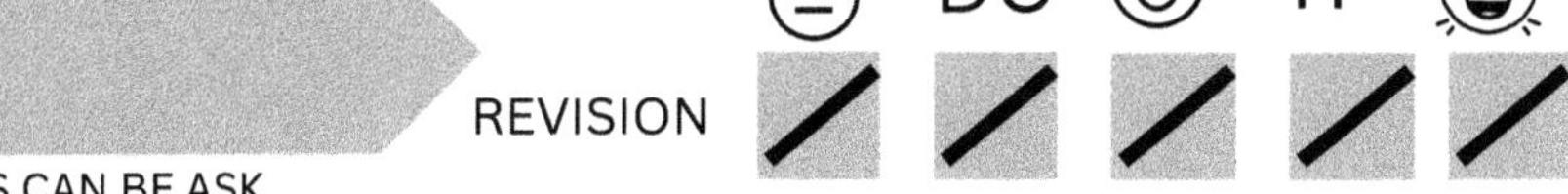

REVISION

QUESTIONS CAN BE ASK

MAIN

KEYWORDS

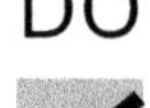

QUESTIONS CAN BE ASK

MAIN

KEYWORDS

REVISION

QUESTIONS CAN BE ASK

MAIN

KEYWORDS

 DO  IT   

REVISION

QUESTIONS CAN BE ASK

MAIN

KEYWORDS

 DO  IT

   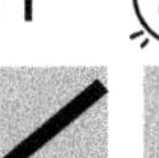 

REVISION

QUESTIONS CAN BE ASK

MAIN

KEYWORDS

QUESTIONS CAN BE ASK

REVISION

MAIN

KEYWORDS

 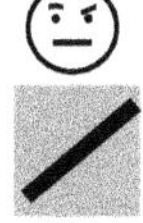  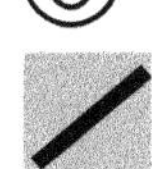   

REVISION

QUESTIONS CAN BE ASK

MAIN

KEYWORDS

REVISION

 DO  IT 

MAIN

KEYWORDS

REVISION    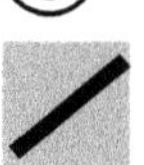     

MAIN

KEYWORDS

 DO 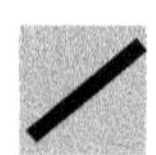 IT 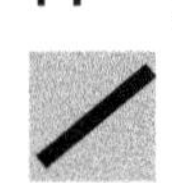

REVISION

QUESTIONS CAN BE ASK

MAIN

KEYWORDS

 REVISION   DO   IT  

MAIN

KEYWORDS

REVISION  DO  IT  

MAIN

KEYWORDS

REVISION

QUESTIONS CAN BE ASK

MAIN

KEYWORDS

QUESTIONS CAN BE ASK

 DO  IT 

REVISION

QUESTIONS CAN BE ASK

MAIN

KEYWORDS

QUESTIONS CAN BE ASK

REVISION

QUESTIONS CAN BE ASK

MAIN

KEYWORDS

MAIN

KEYWORDS

REVISION

QUESTIONS CAN BE ASK

MAIN

KEYWORDS

QUESTIONS CAN BE ASK

QUESTIONS CAN BE ASK

MAIN

KEYWORDS

QUESTIONS CAN BE ASK

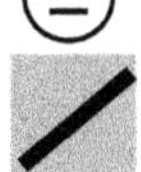

QUESTIONS CAN BE ASK

MAIN

KEYWORDS

 REVISION  DO   IT 

QUESTIONS CAN BE ASK

MAIN

KEYWORDS

REVISION

QUESTIONS CAN BE ASK

MAIN

KEYWORDS

QUESTIONS CAN BE ASK

MAIN

KEYWORDS

REVISION

QUESTIONS CAN BE ASK

MAIN

KEYWORDS

QUESTIONS CAN BE ASK

MAIN

KEYWORDS

  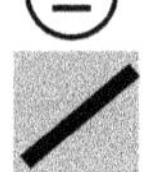    

REVISION

QUESTIONS CAN BE ASK

MAIN

KEYWORDS

QUESTIONS CAN BE ASK

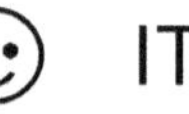

QUESTIONS CAN BE ASK

MAIN

KEYWORDS

QUESTIONS CAN BE ASK

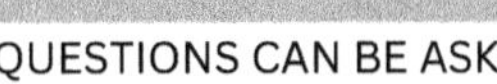   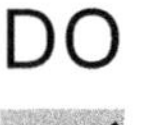    

REVISION

QUESTIONS CAN BE ASK

MAIN

KEYWORDS

REVISION

QUESTIONS CAN BE ASK

MAIN

KEYWORDS

QUESTIONS CAN BE ASK

REVISION

QUESTIONS CAN BE ASK

MAIN

KEYWORDS

QUESTIONS CAN BE ASK

QUESTIONS CAN BE ASK

MAIN

KEYWORDS

REVISION  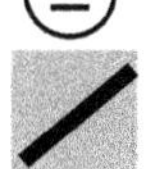     

MAIN

KEYWORDS

REVISION

QUESTIONS CAN BE ASK

MAIN

KEYWORDS

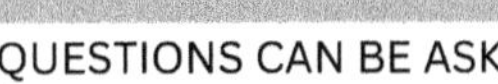

QUESTIONS CAN BE ASK

REVISION  DO   IT 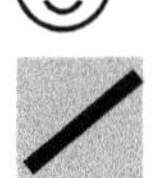  

MAIN

KEYWORDS

REVISION

QUESTIONS CAN BE ASK

MAIN

KEYWORDS

 REVISION   DO  IT 

MAIN

KEYWORDS

QUESTIONS CAN BE ASK
REVISION
DO
IT
MAIN
KEYWORDS
QUESTIONS CAN BE ASK

 DO  IT 

QUESTIONS CAN BE ASK

MAIN

KEYWORDS

REVISION

 DO  IT 

MAIN

KEYWORDS

 DO  IT 

REVISION   

QUESTIONS CAN BE ASK

MAIN

KEYWORDS

QUESTIONS CAN BE ASK

REVISION

DO

IT

MAIN

KEYWORDS

 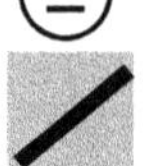     

MAIN

KEYWORDS

QUESTIONS CAN BE ASK

MAIN

KEYWORDS

REVISION  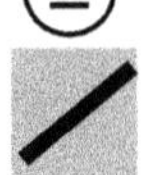     

QUESTIONS CAN BE ASK

MAIN

KEYWORDS

QUESTIONS CAN BE ASK

 REVISION   DO   IT 

MAIN

KEYWORDS

QUESTIONS CAN BE ASK

MAIN

KEYWORDS

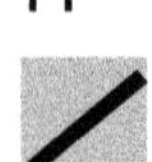

QUESTIONS CAN BE ASK

MAIN

KEYWORDS

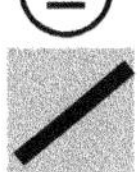

REVISION

QUESTIONS CAN BE ASK

MAIN

KEYWORDS

QUESTIONS CAN BE ASK

QUESTIONS CAN BE ASK
REVISION
DO IT
MAIN
KEYWORDS

 REVISION 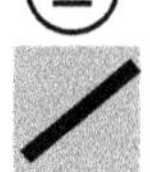 DO  IT 

MAIN

KEYWORDS

REVISION      

MAIN

KEYWORDS

REVISION   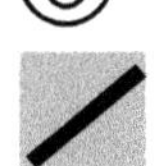   

QUESTIONS CAN BE ASK

MAIN

KEYWORDS

REVISION
DO IT
QUESTIONS CAN BE ASK
MAIN
KEYWORDS

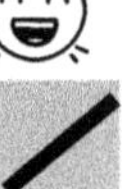

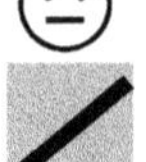

MAIN

KEYWORDS

QUESTIONS CAN BE ASK

MAIN

KEYWORDS

QUESTIONS CAN BE ASK

 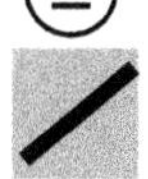    

REVISION

QUESTIONS CAN BE ASK

MAIN

KEYWORDS

REVISION

QUESTIONS CAN BE ASK

MAIN

KEYWORDS

QUESTIONS CAN BE ASK

QUESTIONS CAN BE ASK

MAIN

KEYWORDS

QUESTIONS CAN BE ASK

REVISION  DO 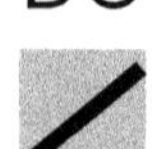 IT   

MAIN

KEYWORDS

REVISION       

MAIN

KEYWORDS

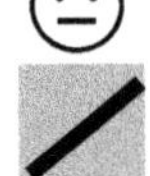

MAIN

KEYWORDS

QUESTIONS CAN BE ASK

MAIN

KEYWORDS

QUESTIONS CAN BE ASK

REVISION

DO

IT

MAIN

KEYWORDS

QUESTIONS CAN BE ASK

MAIN

KEYWORDS

QUESTIONS CAN BE ASK

QUESTIONS CAN BE ASK

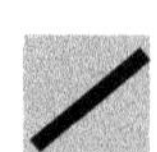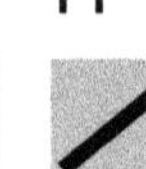

MAIN

KEYWORDS

QUESTIONS CAN BE ASK

REVISION

MAIN

KEYWORDS

QUESTIONS CAN BE ASK

MAIN

KEYWORDS

MIND MAP

MIND MAP

MIND MAP

MIND MAP

MIND MAP

MIND MAP

MIND MAP

MIND MAP

MIND MAP

MIND MAP

MIND MAP

MIND MAP

BLURRING METHOD
REVISION   DATE:
RECALL CONTENT FROM MEMORY
ADD INFORMATION YOU FORGET
ACTIVE RECALL QUSTIONS

BLURRING METHOD

REVISION DATE:

RECALL CONTENT FROM MEMORY

ADD INFORMATION YOU FORGET

ACTIVE RECALL QUSTIONS

BLURRING METHOD   **REVISION**   DATE:

RECALL CONTENT FROM MEMORY

ADD INFORMATION YOU FORGET

ACTIVE RECALL QUSTIONS

BLURRING METHOD

REVISION DATE:

RECALL CONTENT FROM MEMORY

ADD INFORMATION YOU FORGET

ACTIVE RECALL QUSTIONS

BLURRING METHOD

REVISION

DATE:

RECALL CONTENT FROM MEMORY

ADD INFORMATION YOU FORGET

ACTIVE RECALL QUSTIONS

BLURRING METHOD   **REVISION**   DATE:

RECALL CONTENT FROM MEMORY

ADD INFORMATION YOU FORGET

ACTIVE RECALL QUSTIONS

BLURRING METHOD

REVISION   DATE:

RECALL CONTENT FROM MEMORY

ADD INFORMATION YOU FORGET

ACTIVE RECALL QUSTIONS

BLURRING METHOD   **REVISION**   DATE:

RECALL CONTENT FROM MEMORY

ADD INFORMATION YOU FORGET

ACTIVE RECALL QUSTIONS

BLURRING METHOD   **REVISION**   DATE:

RECALL CONTENT FROM MEMORY

ADD INFORMATION YOU FORGET   ACTIVE RECALL QUSTIONS

BLURRING METHOD
REVISION   DATE:
RECALL CONTENT FROM MEMORY
ADD INFORMATION YOU FORGET
ACTIVE RECALL QUSTIONS

BLURRING METHOD

REVISION   DATE:

RECALL CONTENT FROM MEMORY

ADD INFORMATION YOU FORGET

ACTIVE RECALL QUSTIONS

BLURRING METHOD
REVISION   DATE:
RECALL CONTENT FROM MEMORY
ADD INFORMATION YOU FORGET
ACTIVE RECALL QUSTIONS

REVISION

DATE:

RECALL CONTENT FROM MEMORY

ADD INFORMATION YOU FORGET

ACTIVE RECALL QUSTIONS

BLURRING METHOD   **REVISION**   DATE:

RECALL CONTENT FROM MEMORY

ADD INFORMATION YOU FORGET   ACTIVE RECALL QUSTIONS

BLURRING METHOD
REVISION
DATE:
RECALL CONTENT FROM MEMORY
ADD INFORMATION YOU FORGET
ACTIVE RECALL QUSTIONS

BLURRING METHOD

REVISION DATE:

RECALL CONTENT FROM MEMORY

ADD INFORMATION YOU FORGET

ACTIVE RECALL QUSTIONS

BLURRING METHOD   **REVISION**   DATE:

RECALL CONTENT FROM MEMORY

ADD INFORMATION YOU FORGET

ACTIVE RECALL QUSTIONS

BLURRING METHOD

REVISION   DATE:

RECALL CONTENT FROM MEMORY

ADD INFORMATION YOU FORGET

ACTIVE RECALL QUSTIONS

BLURRING METHOD

REVISION　　DATE:

RECALL CONTENT FROM MEMORY

ADD INFORMATION YOU FORGET

ACTIVE RECALL QUSTIONS

BLURRING METHOD   **REVISION**   DATE:

RECALL CONTENT FROM MEMORY

ADD INFORMATION YOU FORGET

ACTIVE RECALL QUSTIONS

REVISION   DATE:

RECALL CONTENT FROM MEMORY

ADD INFORMATION YOU FORGET

ACTIVE RECALL QUSTIONS

BLURRING METHOD

REVISION   DATE:

RECALL CONTENT FROM MEMORY

ADD INFORMATION YOU FORGET

ACTIVE RECALL QUSTIONS

BLURRING METHOD

REVISION   DATE:

RECALL CONTENT FROM MEMORY

ADD INFORMATION YOU FORGET

ACTIVE RECALL QUSTIONS

BLURRING METHOD

REVISION   DATE:

RECALL CONTENT FROM MEMORY

ADD INFORMATION YOU FORGET

ACTIVE RECALL QUSTIONS

BLURRING METHOD **REVISION** DATE:

RECALL CONTENT FROM MEMORY

ADD INFORMATION YOU FORGET

ACTIVE RECALL QUSTIONS

BLURRING METHOD   **REVISION**   DATE:

RECALL CONTENT FROM MEMORY

ADD INFORMATION YOU FORGET   ACTIVE RECALL QUSTIONS

BLURRING METHOD   **REVISION**   DATE:

RECALL CONTENT FROM MEMORY

ADD INFORMATION YOU FORGET

ACTIVE RECALL QUSTIONS

BLURRING METHOD
REVISION
DATE:
RECALL CONTENT FROM MEMORY
ADD INFORMATION YOU FORGET
ACTIVE RECALL QUSTIONS

BLURRING METHOD

REVISION   DATE:

RECALL CONTENT FROM MEMORY

ADD INFORMATION YOU FORGET

ACTIVE RECALL QUSTIONS

BLURRING METHOD

REVISION   DATE:

RECALL CONTENT FROM MEMORY

ADD INFORMATION YOU FORGET

ACTIVE RECALL QUSTIONS

BLURRING METHOD

REVISION   DATE:

RECALL CONTENT FROM MEMORY

ADD INFORMATION YOU FORGET

ACTIVE RECALL QUSTIONS

BLURRING METHOD   **REVISION**   DATE:

RECALL CONTENT FROM MEMORY

ADD INFORMATION YOU FORGET

ACTIVE RECALL QUSTIONS

BLURRING METHOD
RECALL CONTENT FROM MEMORY
REVISION   DATE:
ADD INFORMATION YOU FORGET
ACTIVE RECALL QUSTIONS

BLURRING METHOD   **REVISION**   DATE:

RECALL CONTENT FROM MEMORY

ADD INFORMATION YOU FORGET

ACTIVE RECALL QUSTIONS

BLURRING METHOD **REVISION** DATE:

RECALL CONTENT FROM MEMORY

ADD INFORMATION YOU FORGET

ACTIVE RECALL QUSTIONS

BLURRING METHOD   **REVISION**   DATE:

RECALL CONTENT FROM MEMORY

ADD INFORMATION YOU FORGET

ACTIVE RECALL QUSTIONS

BLURRING METHOD **REVISION** DATE:

RECALL CONTENT FROM MEMORY

ADD INFORMATION YOU FORGET

ACTIVE RECALL QUSTIONS